Sometimes I'm Not Okay

Gabrielle Pilot

BookLeaf Publishing

Presentation by *BookLeaf Publishing*

Web: www.bookleafpub.com

E-mail: info@bookleafpub.com

ISBN : 9789357210669

First edition 2022

To my Momma for pushing me to still do the things I am afraid to do.

PREFACE

It can be easy to feel alone and difficult to find ways to express yourself; it was for me too. Instead, I wrote in private all the things I felt, the things I couldn't say, and the things I meant in the moment that I knew I wouldn't mean forever. It made my feelings real and helped me to release the inner dialogue, tension, and hurt. To you who are reading this, I want you to know:

It's okay to not be fine.
It's okay to not fit in.
It's okay to not be average.
It's okay to not feel normal.
It's okay to not settle for mediocrity.
It's okay to not want to accept the standard.
It's okay to be anxious, lost, unsettled.
It's okay to not be okay; I wasn't either.

Sometimes, I'm still not.

Unlimited

My success shall succeed
That which others believe
Don't limit me with your boundaries
Don't classify me as one like you

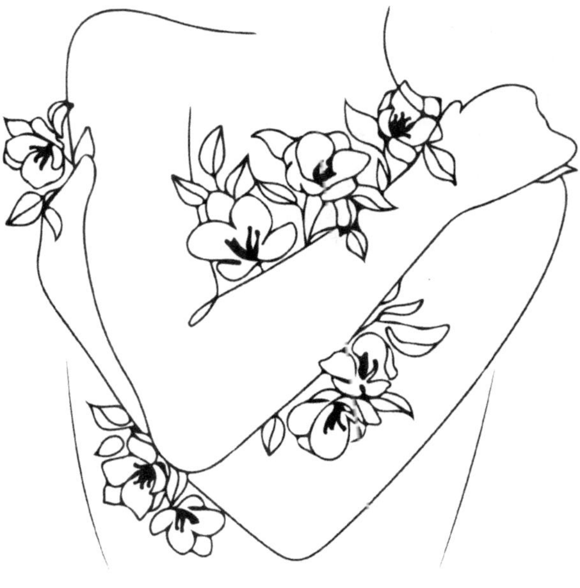

Alter Ego

She's guilty as charged
but here I stand to defend her
her innocence, though I strongly doubt
I feel the need to help her out
looking deep inside of me
it's her standing there looking back at me
pushing me to my limits
fighting against my constraints
refusing to be inhibited
opposites, antonyms we are
yet staring in the mirror
it's her face I see
She may be a contradiction
but she's the only one who
really sees me for me
She's guilty as charged
but here I stand to defend her
her intentions, though others may doubt
I feel the need to help her out

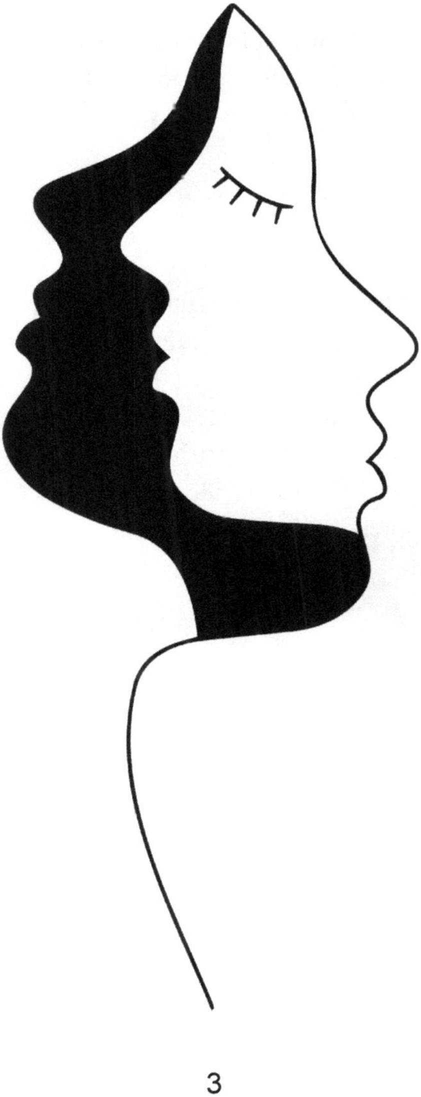

Darkness

Like the shadow that promises to take over,
Like the fear that threatens to smother,
Darkness is coming--
Its advance is intangible,
The coming unseen;
It can't be stopped alone,
The sun will be snuffed out,
Flashlights, candles, no light will linger.
There is only one whose light can push it back,
Go to him, seek him,
Seek the illumination that overcomes the dark.
With him comes victory, triumph;
But the one who stands alone,
The darkness will consume.

Silent I Am Not

Time keeps reminding me
of a forever impending doom
and fallacious little thoughts inside
endlessly generating gloom

Uncaged

Tha dump.
Tha dump.
I want to be free
Tha dump.
Tha dump.
Tha dump.
I need to get out of here
Tha dump. Tha dump. Tha dump. Tha dump.
Why won't you let me go
thadump thadump thadump thadump thadump
Soon I will break free
thadumpthadumpthadumpthadumpthadumpthad
umpthadumpthadumpthadumpthadumpthadump
No more inhibitions

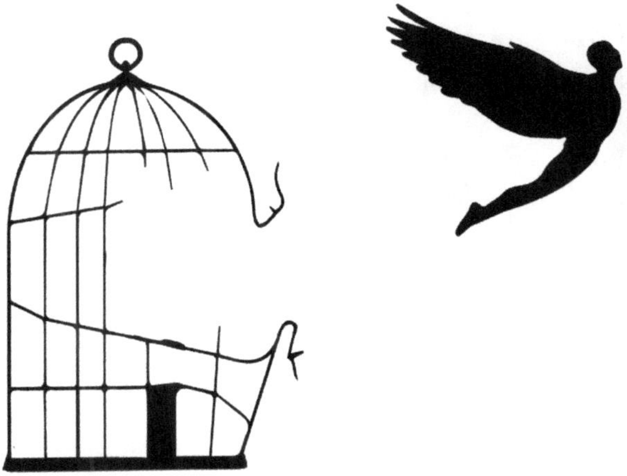

Who I am

I am not invincible.
I am not untouchable.
I am not perfect.

I won't always try my hardest.
I won't always excel.
I won't always make it;
I just might even fail.

I may not be the best.
I may not meet expectations.
I may not stand out in a crowd.

But,

Don't tell me I'm not enough.
Don't tell me who or what to be.
Don't tell me that I can't be me.

Typecast

Don't rate me
Or classify me
Don't count me in.
I'm not a statistic
I won't conform
I'm not the same
I don't fit in.

Predator

It's waiting,
waiting to devour your soul.
It's hungry,
hungry for what will satisfy.
It moves with stealth,
calculating the distance.
It smells your fear,
knows when to make the move.
It will catch you.
Please beware.
Equip yourself for the coming danger.
Prepare now for the attack.
Don't be ignorant prey.
The predator is coming.

Escape

I need to get away
up
up
up
and away
or
down
down
down
beneath ground
where no one can find me
Don't speak
Don't think
Get away
Get away from me.
Pressure
Don't touch me
I need an escape.

Going Over

I keep these insecurities
bottled up inside
crying my heart out
and nobody knows why
because I can't tell them
for fear that they won't understand
and this fear is eating me alive
as I stand on the edge
trying not to fall
down into the depths
of a black hole
reaching out for a ledge
so I can grab hold.

Preface

Am I the only one
who cries all alone
in the back of my closet
when nobody's home?

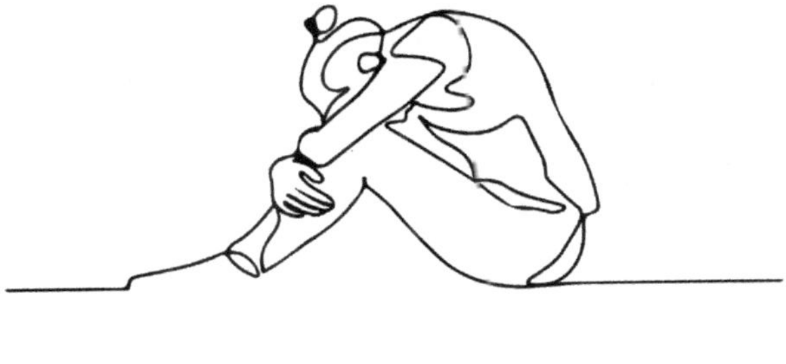

Phobia

I fear the forever passing time
wishing it would all just
Stop.
Instead of
incessantly pushing me forward
when all I want to do is take a step back.
Simultaneously fearing
the inevitable place
where time instantaneously ends
and I am no longer moving forward
but I can't go back either.

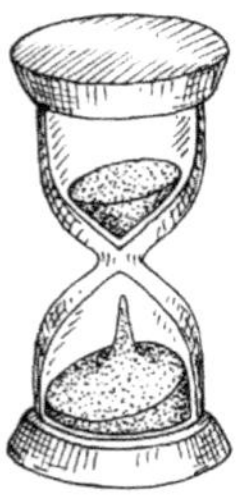

Oppression

There's no point in fighting
I might as well succumb
It knows all my moves
Anticipates every thought
Aiming at an invisible target
I always miss the mark
Battling an unseen opponent
The dark cloud I don't know follows me
Weighing me down
Unbearable pressure
Telling me there isn't any hope
I might as well give up

Coming of Age

Is this what it's supposed to be like?
staying up until four in the morning
eating in the cafeteria with friends
laughing and being silly with the girls
checking out every hot guy that passes
skipping class to get a bit of extra sleep
conversing with people unknown
hanging out all night with someone just met
searching constantly for the definition
looking for that relationship special
reaching out for every chance
grasping for the fleeting opportunities
trying desperately to live to the fullest
attempting to make it the best
throwing out inhibition
finding the balance in between
Is this really as good as it gets?

My Muse is Broken

I feel so inspired,
I want to write this all down.
I have no idea where I'm going,
What I want to write,
Ideas jumbling around;
Struggling to begin,
Oh I hate this!
How I hate this!
I want to write so badly,
I feel so inspired;
If only I knew where to start.

7.25.10

I need a change,
some kind of progress,
to burst me out of this stupor
of self-doubt, hatred,
lack of confidence.

I feel stuck
in a bottomless pit
I can't get out of,
and every second
of everyday,
the top just keeps
getting further away.

This is the most
dissatisfying life
I feel ever lived.
It's no wonder to me,
I want it to be over.

Epilogue

I just can't see
the surface
anymore.

Disappearing Ink

Have you heard the metaphor
'Starting with a clean slate'?

Each day is a new day,
you can always start over
with a blank sheet.

Everyone starting over,
Beginning on a new page;
Never taking time to consider
the paper thrown away.

I fill my sheet left to right
One letter to form a word
One word to form a sentence
One sentence to tell a story
Tracing my way through each day.

The pen touches the paper;
ink to the sheet,
and the wind comes
drying the ink
written on my sheet.

Scrambling to finish,
writing as fast as I can,
trying to fill the page
with my mistakes, my successes,
before the words depart.

So I start

Back at the top,
transcribing on a page
overflowing with yesterdays,
curious at the rationale
of inditing a story that never remains.

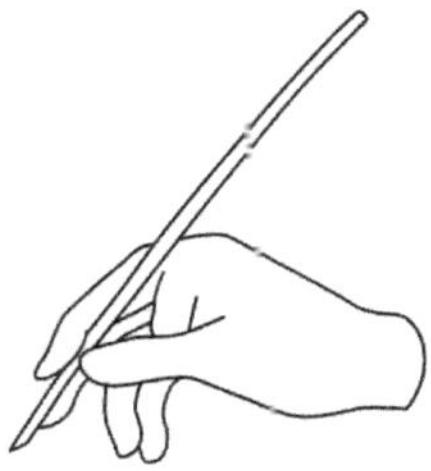

When Inspiration Hits

Leave it all there
So the idea isn't lost
Sleep where I work
Manic
Sleep or create
Create until sleep takes over
Nap and keep going
Nothing to eat
Inspiration feeds hunger
Trash, art side by side
Chaotic, disorganized
All perfectly planned
Don't touch!
You'll ruin the vision
Let the ideas take over
Run until it stops
Take advantage
No interruptions

Forget Me Not

Full of creative energy
bubbling over
exuberantly dripping
My attempt to scream
I EXIST, I AM REAL.
SEE ME, KNOW THAT I WAS HERE.
What will be left?
Will my pictures move?
Tell the story?
I'd burn it all
Just to leave a mark
A lasting mark
So that someone knows
I was here, I was real.
I leave behind pieces
so that I do not lose touch
Everything that I have touched
SHOUTING
I am real, I exist.
I am tangible.
Do not forget.

I am me

I will not be told who I am
Who I should be
I will not be bound by belief

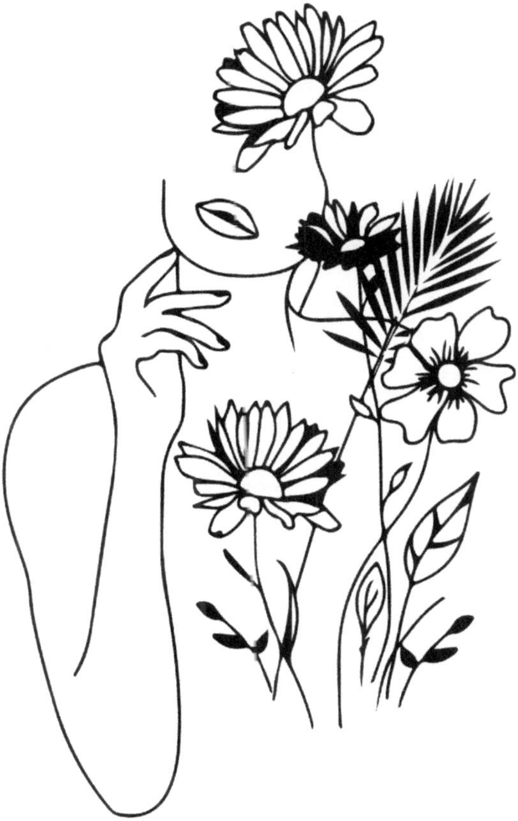

www.ingramcontent.com/pod-product-compliance
Lightning Source LLC
Chambersburg PA
CBHW051758130826
49812CB00033B/1198
9789357210669